Fear and Hope

Fear and Hope

Anna Jordan

Library of Congress Control Number: 2011904531
ISBN: Hardcover   978-1-4568-9112-1
                 Softcover   978-1-4568-9111-4
                 Ebook   978-1-4568-9113-8

This book was printed in the United States of America.

To order additional copies of this book, contact:
Xlibris Corporation
0-800-644-6988
www.xlibrispublishing.co.uk
Orders@Xlibrispublishing.co.uk
301204

I was born in the nineteen sixties in North Yorkshire in the North East of England.

I come from a large family with seven siblings this was a pretty typical situation during this time, we lived in a relatively small three bedroomed house with a set of bunk beds in our bedrooms. There were 2 girls each sharing a bunk topping and tailing and the same with the boys in their room. We were a close family and remain so to this day. We each had our arguments growing up but that's pretty typical with large families.

We were brought up in a small community which consisted of mostly catholic families. We were made to go to church every week at least twice and we were quizzed at home after the service and at school on a Monday morning to make sure we had actually attended the services. We were asked what colour the priests robes were, what was mentioned in the service and even what hymns were sang.

We didn't have much growing up and neither did a lot of families in the area but, we were loved, always clean and well fed.

We were raised to respect older people and call them by their last name like Mr. Jones or Mrs. Smith

My mum had all of us one after another a few of us were not even a year apart, so we all grew up together

There were four girls and four boys and mum and dad.

Our life was very regimented and hectic. We were all given chores to do, mine included ironing for the whole family, all ten of us and its strange to think that I enjoy ironing to this day.

All of us children also worked on milk or paper rounds earning extra cash, if any neighbours wanted us to do odd jobs for them such as cutting their lawns or running errands we would get paid about 50 pence or some sweets depending on what they had we would give the money to our mam for pocket money.

I was the fourth youngest and the fifth oldest but was always small for my age.

I had difficulties speaking and would see a speech therapist regularly for elocution lessons attending them from 5 years of age until I was 12 years old. I was always bullied at school because I was really small, thin, wore glasses, and couldn't speak like everyone else until the age of 12.

At elocution lessons we would say tongue twisting things like peter piper picked a peck of pickled peppers.

I remember my teacher was an elderly woman and she had been doing elocution lessons from being a young girl herself. She did not have any children her self

I also remember I was the only girl in the class, all the rest were boys, I went for 8 years and also went to a normal school about 4 times a week

I loved go to elocution lessons because my mam would pop to the shop on the way home to get me 2 oz of cherry lips and I had to eat them all before we got home, she would always say not tell the others. There were 7 more of us and my mam could not afford a lot.

My mam always looked out for me especially because I was so small and I reminded her of her.

When I started to attend secondary school aged eleven everyone was growing like weeds my mam would say but not me, I was receiving hand me downs from my little sister who was 6 years younger than me. My mam and dad were worried and they ended up taking me to doctors, he said not to worry 'she will grow in her own time' but what my mam and dad didn't know was that I was getting bullied on a daily basis, I was so afraid to tell anyone as I was also targeted by the teachers at my school. I guess they saw me as an easy target given my height and the fact that I was such a timid child. Because of the stress of the bullying and not telling my hair began to fall out so my mam again took me to doctors and this time I was referred to the local hospital to see a specialist they said it was stress and I had to keep off school for about 3 months and when I did go back found out that the children had thrown all of my school books out of the window all on the advice of one of teachers. The same teacher that had targeted me, he had said to the whole school that I wouldn't be returning to the school as I had a disease, I was stood at the side of the assembly hall and I heard this first hand. One of the teachers was telling the children to say a prayer for 'Anna', (me), as she has a terrible disease and would not be returning to our school I stood there in shock as the were throwing by books out of the window in the assembly hall.

A couple of months later the same teachers put boxing gloves on me and also himself and stared to shout 'Anna, go for me' I said 'no sir', so he stared to punch me and all the children were laughing.

Another time we had an assembly and the teacher said 'we are having a knobbly knees contest', he purposely called my name on stage and stated I was the winner, I had not even entered. I remember feeling devastated, ashamed and humiliated; I ran all the way home, I remember it was pouring down with rain and when I arrived home I was soaked through. I told my mam and dad, they went up to the school and sorted the problem out so from my time in secondary school I have never liked bullies or anyone with that intent.

When I left school I started to work as a junior clerk, I loved the job and the excitement of meeting new people, but sadly it was only a training course and didn't last very long, or as long as I would have liked it too.

I then went on to other courses where I met Jack, he was tall, with dark wavy hair and big brown eyes, and we started dating. He was kind and gentle and we were totally compatible, he made me laugh and he made me feel secure. Three years later we had our first child a daughter, Abigail. We married at the local register office, a small ceremony with just family attending and 4 years later we were blessed with our second child, a son Luke. Our family was complete.

It was the best thing in life just being a mum and also a wife, the children were poorly, both asthmatics, but we coped well and every thing was great.

As time went on the children got better in health it was good to know the children didn't need to go to the doctors and the hospital all the time.

Life had been going great, the children had grown and my eldest Abigail had left school and was attending college and my youngest Luke was almost finished secondary school and had plans to study plastering at college.

We decided to move to a bigger property closer to my mother and sisters as we were living quite far away from all that I knew really but not long after moving in our new home I regretted the decision.

You see I met this young girl she had four babies all of which where under four years of age she didn't have much so I opened my heart to her and she told me all about her life, she had a drug addiction which I did not know about at the time but I am the sort of person that couldn't say to the girl I didn't want to know her because my heart went out for the children. I fed all of them breakfast every morning and tea every evening and I also took then home, bathed the children, put them in their pyjamas and put them to bed, only when the children were asleep I went home and I thought to myself the children have been fed and they would be ok. What I didn't know was that the girls' sisters were also taking drugs and they would turn up at the girls' house at 2 o'clock in the morning and bang on the door, waking everybody in the house and all of them would be doing drugs around the children.

One particular morning the girl turned up very early at my door before I'd even set off for work, she was in a terrible state, I asked her what was wrong, she stated that the little boy, her youngest not even a year old had taken some drugs. Not knowing what to say and in a state of shock myself I said what are you talking about? Inviting her in she proceeded to tell me about her sisters, they were both dug addicts and to pay for them they were both prostitutes, one of them, she didn't know which had dropped a little bit of heroin on the bed and the little one had automatically put it in his mouth.

I told her to take the child straight to the hospital and get him checked over.

So off she went, when I had finished work that evening she was at my door, she said the doctor said he was fine and had a touch of flu.

I honestly to this day do not think she had actually taken him.

Life was changing; I had a job that I loved as a care worker in the community. my children where 14 and 18 and one day as I was on my way to work I heard a voice shout 'smack head', not thinking anything of it but being naturally inquisitive I looked around, I didn't see anyone so just shrugged it off, never in a million years did I think it was aimed at me.

Every day from then I heard same voice say the same thing so I thought to myself some one is playing silly games.

Life was very busy for me in February, 1999 but I was content.

I lived opposite my mum and had a lot of family living around me.

I was happily married with two lovely children, daughter Abigail was almost 18 and my son Luke was 14, when I went to bed at I would look across the road at my mums house and she would be there, in her bedroom looking at me and waving goodnight. I was so happy.

Why it all went wrong, I don't know I still ask myself. After almost 8 years of despair, what did I do that was so bad that I deserved my horrendous nightmare?

I will try and explain how it all began, you see I met a young single mum Sally; she had 4 young children named Stephen, Mark, Paul and Lee. She started to talk about her life, and how hard things were for her

I felt so sorry for her and her young children. if she needed anything she knew she could come to my home, be it a lending hand or a shoulder to cry on.

A couple of days past and one night a knock came at my door, standing there with the children in tow was Sally she had no food or milk for the children so I brought her and the children in, fed them and took them home but the next day she was at my door again, I didn't mind knowing that the children were being fed. I prepared a meal for sally and the children and said see you later as I had to go to work but I will be back at dinner time.

I just got home and Sally was on my door step waiting for me she said I have something to tell you, she said she was a drug addict i was very shocked, I didn't know what drugs were. She said please can you help me get off the drugs for the sake of my children? I said ok, I will try so I got on the phone and sorted time out with a drug worker. I was pleased with myself, helping her change her life for the better for the sake of her beautiful children who I'd become really attached too.

I will try and explain how it all began and how it is still ongoing. What little faith I have in people who said they would help but never did and how it has affected my whole existence and that of my family around me.

I remember the first day quite vividly. i was walking to the local shops and I heard a female voice "smack head", I turned to see who it was and no-one was there. This happened everyday for a long time and i thought someone was playing stupid games so I ignored it.

By this time I had a job that I loved I was a care worker in the community and i loved helping elderly people in their own homes. I travelled all around my local area on my bicycle.

One day I was cycling to work as normal and suddenly i was pushed from my bike and a woman, who I had never seen before was screaming smack head at me. She punched me over and over again and yanked at my hair. i was frightened and in shock and very upset. As quick as the attack began it was over and the woman walked off. I remember picking myself up from the floor and getting back on my bicycle, wiping the dirt and tears from my face trying to compose myself. I didn't want to let the elderly people i cared for down so I carried on to work, crying and at a loss to know why this person had done this to me.

I rang the police on my mobile phone and explained what had happened and they said to call in the police station later on in the day and they would take a statement

I did go in to the police station but that same day there was a murder in the town and every available police officer was busy. They said I would have to come back another time, as my attack was not classed as urgent.

Unfortunately this was the beginning of the daily physical and mental abuse I would receive from this woman whom I hadn't met until that day

Every morning i would get up, get ready for work and set off on my bicycle and everyday the woman came from nowhere and punched me in the back or would pull my hair. I carried on with my daily life but I was beginning to get very, very frightened at what she would do next.

I told no-one of my ordeal. I was too ashamed to tell anyone that I was afraid

One day I was going to the local shops and a man stopped me, he accused me of shouting at his mother, I had no idea what he was talking about, j had never raised my voice to anyone. The woman who attacked me and been attacking me frequently was his mother. I said to him I had no idea what he was talking about, I don't know him and then he spat all over me, it was the most disgusting thing and is the most disgusting thing that anyone could do to another person.

It was dripping off my clothes and hair and I had to stop myself from crying. I ran all the way home and got straight into the shower and scrubbed and scrubbed until I was red raw, I felt totally humiliated and so dirty. I burned the clothes and coat I was wearing as I could not face the thought of wearing them again. I was beginning to feel physically sick with fear.

Apparently the woman who attacked me lived in the same road as me, on the opposite side, a little further along the road. I realised she was able to watch me coming and going on a daily basis

I stared to cycle in different directions to avoid her bullying but she always seemed to be there, and always punching me from behind. It got that I expected the physical abuse and the only respite I got was when she was on holiday No-one needed to tell me she was away, I just knew because there was no abuse

One day sally ran to tell my mam what she had heard people around the shop talking about.

They were all talking about the woman's son and the disgusting incident when he had spat all over me.

So when I popped over the road to see if my mum was ok after work one day, my mam said "can I ask you some thing?" I said "yes, what's wrong", my mam then said what sally had been told, I was shocked to learn that people had seen what had happened and did nothing about this, no one wanted to know, but they were quick to talk about it around the local shop.

I said to my mam she was wrong, sally had heard wrong, I said I didn't know what she was talking about but I think she knew I was lying and trying to protect her.

There had to be some thing wrong with me, I was not myself any more I went home prepared the tea and i could not understand why that woman's son had do this to me. I was so ashamed because i told lies to my mam for the first time in my life but I couldn't tell my mam because she was ill, you see she had a bad heart. She had been diagnosed with diabetes many years earlier but as time went by she had developed other health problems another reason I was worried about telling her due to her heart problems and the stress it would bring upon her.

Her attacks on me carried on almost daily for months.

Another day I will never forget I was going to work and I was walking with a young woman called Bella who has leaning difficulties.

I thought I would accompany her to the centre she attended when suddenly the woman attacked me again from behind.

I fell across my bike and she kept punching me and screaming abuse.

Bella shouted at the woman, "Don't hit my Anna" and the woman screamed at her to shut up, calling her a "mong".

I was upset for Bella, she was crying and asking why the woman was being nasty, i couldn't answer her; I only wished

I could have, for her sake and mine.

I kept asking myself why she was doing this to me. I hadn't even know her before all this began.

I was nervous and frightened all the time. I began to padlock my front gate as she started to come down to my house when she knew I was alone.

Sometimes I was too frightened to call over the road to my mam's house in case she got to me before I reached the house. I would sit in my house alone and cry.

My house became my prison.

When I did go to my mams house, my mam would look at me and say "what's the matter Anna?, you are changing, tell me what's troubling you"; I would say there was nothing wrong, I just felt under the weather but I knew the way she looked at me that she knew there had to be a problem.

I was normally happy go lucky, and always had a joke with my mam but this no longer happened.

I wanted my mam to give me a cuddle and reassure me and I would cry with my head on her lap but I couldn't tell her what was happening because she was poorly and had her own troubles.

I didn't tell my husband Jack or my sisters or brothers, I just kept it to myself and hoped it would stop.

I stopped going to the local shops. I only went shopping if my husband Jack or my sisters were there with me.

I didn't go into town anymore or the local mall and I didn't go to my local church as it meant passing her house.

I didn't feel safe anywhere.

I had to go to work, so the punches, kicks and hair pulling went on and on.

I felt I couldn't turn to anyone of the shame it would impose on me.

I had always detested bullies but I never thought at the age of 37 that I would be so hurt physically and mentally by another woman who appeared to be in her late 50's

The woman was large and stocky, quite frightening to look at and she seemed to haunt even my dreams.

I couldn't get away from her.

After almost 18 months I couldn't cope any longer and had to resign from my job.

I had to say goodbye to my old people who I had enjoyed working for so much and i was devastated.

But I just couldn't carry on being beaten every time I left home to go to work.

Why wouldn't she leave me alone?

I began to think that if i changed my appearance she wouldn't recognise me so i virtually stopped eating.

At the time I cooked not just for my family. I also cooked tea for my mam, sister and brother and would take it across the road on a large tray.

My husband jack would ask me where my tea was and I would say that I had already eaten but I actually hadn't eaten at all.

To be quite honest the thought of the woman made me physically sick and the thought of putting any food in my mouth was stomach churning I lived on coffee with a lot of sugar, cigarettes and a small square of chocolate daily.

That's all I could mange.

My weight was dropping dramatically.
I wore extra clothes underneath to hide my size.

I started to take laxatives to lose weight as I still thought that the woman wouldn't recognise me if I changed my appearance.

I even dyed my hair the only one who knew something was drastically wrong with me was my mother but I thought by keeping it from her she wouldn't worry.

I should have known my mam was worrying about me because she didn't know what the problem was.

She tried to coax it out of me many times but I would laugh it off, telling her not to worry and say nothing was wrong.

When I went home I would try to act as normal as possible but when everyone was in bed I would get up in the early hours and sit and cry a million tears and beg God to take me.

My life was over; I couldn't bear the torment of this woman's actions any longer.

There seemed to be no end to this woman's cruelty.

One summers evening I was sitting on my mam's neighbours front, just inside the garden.

Her daughter came out of the house with two cups of tea one for each of us, we were chatting.

As I put the cup to my mouth it smashed into my face.

The woman must have spotted me chatting and made her way to where I was and attacked me without warning. I didn't even see her coming.

I wasn't aware of my injuries at the time, she had hold of me and dragging me towards her as she walked backwards and she fell in the garden hedge with me on top of her but she wouldn't leave go of me punching me in the head and pulling my hair I was dizzy, I couldn't get free until someone pulled me off the woman she had to leave go of me.

At the time my mam was in her bedroom as she had a broken leg and she heard the screams, she shouted for my sister Nat to help me. In the meantime, the police were called and someone had gone to my house and told my husband Jack that this woman was attacking his wife, me, so Jack came running to see what was happening. When he saw I was being attacked, he went mad and told the police to put that woman in prison. and then the police turned on my husband ordering him to get in his house, he said to them to sort this out and the next thing jack was taken away and put in the police cells all because he stood up for me, and yet again she got away with this attack and jack got fined from the police for standing up for me. I couldn't believe it, all my husband had done was ask the police to sort this woman out and it seemed they had taken her side even spraying tear gas in my husbands' eyes.

Their excuse for this injustice, because children were present and he shouldn't shout or swear, I'm sure my attacker wasn't thinking about my children when she was attacking me, justice?

I think not!

My sister pulled the woman off me.

She had knocked four of my teeth out.

My glasses had been forced into my eyelid, which needed 7 stitches and my nose was fractured.

The police escorted the woman home and charged her with actual bodily harm but not before she attempted to kick out at my mother, who had slowly made her way downstairs to try and help me even though she was in no condition too.

That, to me, summed up what type of person this woman was, and making me realise she would stop at nothing to try and hurt me.

I was taken to hospital and was in shock for a long time.

After this attack, I more or less hid away from everyone and everything.

I only ventured out to see my mam, but I didn't even feel safe doing that and my visits became less frequent.

By this time I believe I was almost out of my mind.

I remember thinking I will have to take my own life because I couldn't carry on like this any longer and I would be free.

I couldn't face the thought of going to court and having to face this woman, I was absolutely terrified.

I got up about 2:00 am and locked myself in the bathroom.

I sat behind the bathroom door and wrote a letter to my husband and my children and my mam explaining why I had to take my life and that this was the only way i would have peace.

I had lots of tablets next to me and started to take them suddenly my daughter tried the door and said, 'is that you mam?' and I stopped. I thought to myself what sort of mother would do this to her children; I was devastated at the thought of my children having no mam.

This woman had almost won.

The next day I went to see my mam and told her everything.

What I had suffered for the last 18 months and what I almost did the day before.

She was heartbroken and begged me to move away.

She supported me all the way and this decision did indeed save my life.

That night I was in the bath.

I always locked the bathroom door but this night I had forgot and my husband Jack walked in.

He was so shocked at the sight of my emaciated body he just stood speechless.

I had to tell him everything.

He agreed we would start again somewhere else and said the courts would deal with the woman for what she did.

How wrong we were.

My main witness, the neighbour I was chatting to when the assault happened, wouldn't come to court she said she was frightened of the possible intimidation and harassment from the woman, as she still had to live there.

The woman got away with her assault on me.

The police officers and victim support were disgusted but could do nothing, because of my attackers' age.

I felt so let down and frightened, my weight plummeted.

I was literally a nervous wreck.

We moved a long way away from where we were but the loneliness was unbearable and again I decided to end my life but yet again it was my daughter who inadvertently stopped me, although at the time she hadn't known it took three long years for me to settle.

I was sad that I had to take my son out of his school and couldn't visit my mam but she came with my sister Nat to visit as often as she could.

My son found it very difficult to adjust in his new school.

My daughter and son had to leave their lifelong friends behind and to this day I still guilty as it is obvious this affected them more than I realised.

When I moved into my new house I weighed 4 st. 4 lbs, I didn't realise I was so thin.

I never looked in the mirror I had since lost my self esteem and confidence.

I used to stay in all day and not even bother to get dressed; I had to see my doctor regularly.

He gave me anti-depressants, sleeping tablets, basically anything I wanted, but all I wanted was that woman to stop hurting me.

I didn't trust anyone anymore but eventually I started to speak with a neighbour who lived opposite.

She was a good listener and little by little I told her what had happened.

We became very close and if I needed someone to talk to or confide in, she was there.

She still is, in fact, it's my friend whom is putting this down on paper for me.

After a while I decided I would have to be strong and go out.

I was shaking with fear but I thought I had to make an effort and try.

I went into my favourite shop in the town but as I was started to leave the woman was outside the door watching me. She was with a group of other women and she started to taunt me and shouted for me, she was waiting for me to come out.

The staff saw what was happening and took me out the back to calm me down.

I had to stay there until the woman got tired of waiting and disappeared, but I had to wait for my husband Jack and son Luke to be called by phone to come and collect me.

Needless to say I have never been into the town centre since.

Over the years I got letters from her solicitors accusing me of trying to knock her down in the car (I didn't drive) and harassment and warning me I would have to go to court if it didn't stop.

These letters were sent to my mother's address, as obviously the woman didn't know where I lived.

I hadn't been to my mothers for almost three years so the woman was lying but how could I prove otherwise?

How is it possible that a solicitor can just take someone's word that something had happened without proof?

Every time I received a letter I felt like my whole life was falling apart again.

Every part of my body would shake with fright, and then I couldn't eat or sleep again.

She was slowly killing me without even putting another hand on me.

Then i received a letter from her solicitor at my home.

I was frantic, how had she found out where I lived.

This time she had accused me of trying to knock her and her grandson over.

I showed my friend the letter and she advised me to go to see a solicitor myself and explain to them what had been happening.

My solicitor investigated the matter with the police and other agencies and decided that I should take this woman to court for an injunction, for my own safety.

The day I went to court with my solicitor was horrific; I was terrified and physically shaking.

I had to stand in the same room as her but I kept my eyes on the judge the whole time.

The whole time, what felt like forever, I was shaking from head to toe and it was pretty obvious I was terrified, I did not know what to expect.

She had to make a promise to the court that she would keep away from my home and me, but the shocking part was the promise was for only 3 months and also I had to promise her, yet I had no done anything to her.

I asked my solicitor why only 3 months and why do I have to promise her anything, she said the barrister who had been appointed for me felt I would not be strong enough to go though the ordeal of a full injunction at that time as I was not physically or mentally strong enough to handle a cross examination from her solicitor so this was the best solution.

I thought at least I had been given a little breathing space and I had made a stand and taken legal action.

I went to my mother's house after this promise but I was escorted and in a car, I was never alone as I still didn't feel safe.

The first time she saw me in my husband jacks car she ran into the road and threw stones at the car.

Every time I visited my mothers house the woman always knew and would run out at the car and shout abuse or throw something.

In the end whoever I went with, I would bend down in the passenger seat or back seat of the car so she couldn't see me.

An odd time on my return home from my mothers I kept looking in the cars wing mirror, I just couldn't shake off the feeling that we were being followed.

My husband tried to reassure me and said why would anyone want to follow us.

It turned out that this woman had followed me home, she admitted as much to the local housing officer, when she had gone in to complain about someone else.

She said she followed me, apparently to satisfy her curiosity, that I did actually live at that address' the housing officer' I have been told since was aware of her written promise to the court, and should have reported this immediately to the police and they would have acted upon it.

However the officer didn't deem it necessary.

So yet again this woman got away with her actions and left me distraught at the knowledge that she now knew exactly where I lived.

She reported me to the Social Security department and housing Department saying I was fraudulently claiming benefits, which they accepted as being malicious, although they did have to investigate the allegation.

It just seemed ironic to me that I wouldn't have been on any benefits at all but for the actions of this same woman who caused my illness.

By this time she seemed to have an obsession with all my family, mainly my mother, sister and one brother.

She would shout abuse outside my mother's house, she attacked two of my sisters at different times and my brother was physically pushed from his motorbike just as he was riding it away from the house.

Her son smashed my mother's windows one Boxing Day morning.

He was arrested and admitted the offence and was ordered to pay compensation but my mother never received any money from him at all.

Each one of my family, over a period of time, were stopped or visited by the police to have their vehicles and documentation checked.

My brother James was accused of stealing motorbikes, which again was proven to be more malicious lies.

After all this time I still feel as though it was that all this was happening to my family because I didn't stand up to this woman at the very beginning.

My heart ached for my mam, she wasn't well at all and the situation seemed to be making her worse.

I stay away for totally, thinking that if i didn't visit anymore the woman wouldn't harass my mam or family.

I missed them all so much but i thought it better to stay away for my sake and theirs.

One night I got a phone call to say my mam had been taken very ill.

My husband and I rushed to her home to find an ambulance outside.

The paramedics were lifting my mother into the ambulance and the woman was stood opposite laughing and clapping.

One of the paramedics thought the woman was mentally ill to carry on the way she was.

My mam stayed in hospital for over two weeks she had a weak heart and she seemed to be getting better, I think and still do she was making improvements in her health while being away from that woman and all the stress and harassment she brought.

I prayed everyday for her to get better and there seemed to be a slight improvement.

She was discharged.

A week later, I received another phone call; my mam had been taken to the hospital.

I went to the hospital to visit one day and my world suddenly fell apart.

We called in a room and the doctor said my mam had two weeks to live.

When i saw my mam, she looked well and the next minute she looked around her bed, the curtains were round, I was hiding behind the hospital curtains and my mam said "Where is Anna?" I said "I'm here mam" so I went to see her. She turned to face me, she said I love you all and then she passed away.

My best friend, my life, my rock, my mam gone and I would never see her again.

I was destroyed.

I loved her so much

I don't remember much that followed apart from my best friend Nicola driving me to my mother's house the next day.

As we were coming away the woman ran from her house, picked something from the ground and went to throw it at the car.

My friend was so angry; she stopped the car and just growled at the woman through the car window.

It seemed to do the trick, because the woman dropped the stones and went back in.

I nicknamed Nicola the 'rottweiller' after that.

Apparently in the local club, where the woman often frequented she was seen dancing and laughing saying,

'The old . . . . is dead;' my mam was only 66 when she passed away, not much older than her.

How could anyone be so brutal to act in this way but then nothing surprised me with this woman anymore?

The day of the funeral we had to pass the woman's house as the church was at the end of the road.

As we passed with our beloved mother she was at her window waving, laughing and clapping.

Where was God, why was he letting this happen, where was the justice in the world.

At least she couldn't torment my lovely mam anymore. I knew she would finally have the peace she deserved.

8 months after my mother had passed away, my bother Lee died. He was only 45 years old and had a daughter aged only four whom he adored, his only child. Even his funeral did not go peacefully; again she was stood watching, with a face so full of hatred, waving, clapping and laughing as the hearse with my beloved brother in drove to the church for the service.

I was left feeling so angry that after all the times my mam and sister had reported her to the local council and the police for doing terrible things but all to no avail.

My sister had even installed CCTV and shown the videos of her harassment to the police but nothing happened.

The council had even asked them to complete diaries on a daily basis, but again nothing happened

After providing all evidence to the council and the police suddenly all videos and diaries have been 'mislaid'.

My mam's last few years on this earth were not peaceful because of this woman.

I will always feel bitter towards those who weren't prepared to help and I will never, not in a million years ever forgive

This woman for what she has done to me, my mother and my family.

After leaving the area, Sally returned to using drugs, she no longer has her children living with her and also according to rumours was paid to make a statement against me but was not used as evidence against me as it was proved she had lied. I had actually helped her take care of her children and was a good friend to her—I will never trust her again and actually feel sorry for her and her children.

I also discovered that I was targeted by this woman as I was mistaken for someone else; the lady who I was mistaken for is actually Sally's sister who looks from the back as I use to look all those years ago.

Because of this woman's actions I am now under a dietician for anorexia, I suffer with bouts of severe depression, I am extremely nervous and can never be alone.

I am an outpatient at our local mental health hospital; I have weekly visits to a very caring and understanding community psychiatric nurse.

I have to visit my doctor regularly, have appointments with a dietician, have had counselling and it just goes on and on.

Almost two years have passed since my beloved mother left us and still this woman is harassing my family and me.

She is now taking the registration numbers of every car that stops outside my mother's house, where my sister and brothers still live.

Why? We don't know and again a month ago the windows of my mother's house were smashed again. We know she is paying local drug users to do this but even having proof does not bring resolution.

She reported me and sister again to the Social Security office but this time we were told it was obviously a vendetta and this would most definitely be dealt with.

Will I ever get my sanity back? Have a normal life? Will I ever be able to grieve properly for my beautiful mam?

If justice eventually prevails, maybe I will.

But how much time will have to pass, how many more years of my life and my family's life will be destroyed before this eventually happens?

This is what I have suffered:

Physical Bullying

Personal Belongings destroyed

Punching, Hitting, Kicking Pushing

Physical Contact.

Feeling humiliated

Feeling dirty

Hurt

Pain

Loss

Moving from one house to another and always been stalked.

Always looking over you shoulder expecting an attack

Loss of friends

To this day the woman has not stopped but no-one wants to know, all they say is how can we solve it after all these years? But how can't they stop it because it's still on going, so for me it would be classed as a different incident so they should sort the problem out.

My sister Nat has filled all the sheets she was given from the council everyday for all these years and all they keep saying is just do what you have been doing.

This will not sort problem out because all the other sheets suddenly get mislaid

My other sister Billy got the police to go round that woman's house after she had been abusing my sister so why can't anyone help my sister Nat?

She doesn't want to move home and I don't blame her really, why should she, it what this woman wants. It's the home we all grew up in and it holds a lot of memories for her and all of us.

The police know that it is this woman that has caused the trouble but they say because it happened to one sister it's a totally different incident but it's not to me because it is on going abuse.

I was watching the television a few months back and saw a breaking news bulletin and heard the story of a single mother that was targeted by a group of youths, she took her own life. I was thinking to myself how that was almost me.

Why is this sort of harassment not dealt with when it is reported? I really felt for the lady and all that she had to go through, I know exactly how it feels; the only difference is the abuse I suffered was from a woman who was in her fifties when this all started which is unheard of. She is still abusing my family members today and is well into her sixties and we still have no resolution.

By Anna Jordan

www.ingramcontent.com/pod-product-compliance
Lightning Source LLC
Chambersburg PA
CBHW050346290526
45785CB00006B/2663